Peggy Barton

THE JOHN BAPT

JOHN THE BAPTIST

Deseret Book Company   Salt Lake City, Utah   1978

Library of Congress Cataloging in Publication Data

Barton, Peggy, 1931-
  John the Baptist.

  SUMMARY: Presents the life and work of John the
Baptist who predicted the coming of the Messiah and
baptized Jesus. Explains how the Priesthood of Aaron
was conferred upon Joseph Smith and Oliver Cowdery.
  1. John the Baptist—Juvenile literature. 2. Prophets
—Palestine—Biography—Juvenile literature. [1. John
the Baptist. 2. Prophets. 3. Church of Jesus Christ of
Latter-day Saints] I. Title.

BS2456.B29   225.9′2′4 [B]   78-23616
ISBN O-87747-727-2

CONTENTS

ZACHARIAS WAS A VERY OLD MAN. HE HAD LIVED A LONG AND HAPPY LIFE AS A PRIEST OF THE FAMILY OF AARON SERVING IN THE TEMPLE. HE LOVED to watch the people come with their smiling faces and their offerings.

There was one desire Zacharias and his old wife Elisabeth had prayed for over and over again through the years. This was to have a child. But their prayers had not been answered. Undoubtedly, as Zacharias observed the parents with their children in the temple courtyard, he longed for the son he believed that he and Elisabeth could never have.

One day the angel Gabriel appeared to Zacharias as he was near the golden altar in the temple. Imagine his surprise when the angel said, "Thy prayer is heard; and thy wife Elisabeth shall bear thee a son, and thou shalt call his name John." (Luke 1:13.)

Zacharias was filled with doubt and amazement as Gabriel went on speaking. The angel promised that the baby would grow strong and be great in the sight of the Lord, and that he would turn many people to God and help them to prepare themselves to receive the Messiah when He came. The angel told Zacharias that John should use neither wine nor strong drink, and that he would be filled with the Holy Ghost from the time of his birth.

"How could I have a son?" Zacharias asked, doubting that at his age he would at last become a father. "For," he said, "my wife is old, long past the time to bear children."

And the angel answered, saying, "Thou shalt be dumb, and not able to speak, until the baby is born, because you do not believe my words." And at that moment Zacharias did lose his power to speak. This would be a constant reminder to him that he should trust in God and His wisdom and do His will without questioning.

The people outside the temple wondered why Zacharias was so long inside, and when he finally came out, he could not tell them. Not one sound came from his mouth. He realized that the angel's words were indeed true, and that no one would hear his voice until his little son was born. And he believed that his son would prepare the way for the coming of Jesus Christ, and that he must be named John instead of Zacharias after himself.

With joy, Zacharias and Elisabeth anxiously awaited the birth of their first and only child of whom the Savior would say, "No greater prophet has ever been born of woman."

Mary's good news

SIX MONTHS AFTER GABRIEL HAD VISITED ZACHARIAS IN THE TEMPLE, THE ANGEL RETURNED TO EARTH AND APPEARED TO ELIZABETH'S YOUNG COUSIN MARY, WHO lived in Nazareth, a city of Galilee. He addressed her, saying, "Hail, thou that art highly favoured, the Lord is with thee: blessed art thou among women." (Luke 1:28.)

Gabriel went on to tell her that she had been chosen to

become the mother of God's own Son on earth, Jesus Christ. Mary was probably even more surprised than Zacharias had been when the angel appeared to him. But she listened to the words of Gabriel and did not doubt. She was filled with wonderment when the angel said that her elderly cousin Elisabeth was also to have a son.

Immediately, Mary decided to leave for a visit to the hill country where Zacharias and Elisabeth lived. She wanted to rejoice with them over her news, news that would change the destiny of all mankind. She longed for the cool green comfort of the mountains, the cold rush of streams and gently blowing breezes, the familiar olive trees, the vines, goats, and sheep.

When Mary arrived at her cousin's house, Elisabeth exclaimed, "Blessed art thou among women. . . . Whence is this to me, that the mother of my Lord should come to me?" (Luke 1:42-43.)

And at her words, the baby in Elisabeth's body leapt for joy! Elisabeth had been inspired to know that Mary was to bear the Son of God even before Mary told her. As the two women embraced, they praised their Heavenly Father for their great blessings and wondered at the parts they would play in the most important event in the history of the world.

For about three months, Mary stayed at the home of Elisabeth and Zacharias, sharing with them the excitement that the births of their sons would bring. Mary and Elisabeth must have humbly wondered, *Will they be like other babies? How do we live with a prophet and the Son of God as they grow to manhood?*

After a long visit, Mary returned to her home and Elisabeth entered the last few days before John was born.

THE SON OF ELISABETH AND ZACHARIAS WAS BORN! THE BABY—BATHED, RUBBED WITH OIL, AND WRAPPED IN SWADDLING CLOTHES—WAS placed in his father's arms by the midwife as was the custom. How happy the old couple were with the healthy, boisterous newborn who had been sent to them for their special care! Could they doubt the greatness of God when this child was one of His miracles?

On the eighth day following the baby's birth, friends, neighbors, and relatives crowded into the home of Zacharias, for this was the time of naming and circumcision. Not one of those in the little room had really believed that the old priest and his wife would bring forth a son because of their age. But none could deny the presence of the lusty baby boy lying on his little bed near the window.

Everyone thought that, of course, the child would be named after his father, especially since Zacharias had waited so long for a son.

Elisabeth objected. "No," she declared, "his name must be John."

Neighbors and relatives were puzzled. *Has the birth been so hard for her that she is confused and tired?* they wondered. So they summoned Zacharias.

The old man still could not speak. The Bible indicates he may not have been able to hear either, for those gathered for the naming made signs to ask what the baby should be called.

Zacharias motioned for a writing tablet to be brought and he scrawled in large bold letters, HIS NAME IS JOHN. And the people marveled.

As soon as he had written these words, Zacharias regained his speech and began to praise God, telling of the wonderful future in store for his son. "And thou, child," he said, "shalt be called the prophet of the Highest: for thou shalt go before the face of the Lord to prepare his ways; to give knowledge of salvation unto his people by the remission of their sins." (Luke 1:76-77.)

The friends and relatives gathered in the little room were amazed at the words of the priest. They were surprised that his speech had been restored so suddenly, and were shocked at the message he foretold. Did Zacharias mean that a little child could actually prepare the way of the Lord? Could this baby from the house of David help free his people from fear and bondage?

They hurried to tell their friends and families of the wonders they had witnessed. Soon the story of the birth of the baby to the old couple, Zacharias' loss of speech and its miraculous return, the prophecies—all were repeated in the uplands of Judea.

"What will the baby become?" the people asked each other. "Who can deny now that an angel really visited Zacharias?"

Everyone hearing the story was amazed and filled with wonderment about what the future would mean to the baby John and the people of Israel. Even in their amazement they could not possibly understand the true miracle that had been brought about by the hand of the Lord.

THERE IS A STORY TOLD
BY THE OLD ONES IN
ISRAEL THAT WHEN GOD
CREATED THE EARTH HE
SENT OUT TWO ANGELS,
EACH WITH A BAG OF ROCKS.
One angel scattered the rocks in his bag all over the world.
The other angel dropped all of the rocks in his bag in one
place—and that place is called Israel.

Few really believe this tale, but all who have traveled to
the land where John was born and grew to manhood know
that the soil is thin and unyielding. Because of the rocky fields
it is not possible to use modern farm equipment in Judea
until stones are removed by hand and piled into walls. Some
of these walls were begun two thousand years ago; they act as
boundaries in addition to terracing the land so that some
water might stay on the arid soil. The sight of a man holding
a wooden plow behind a struggling horse is the same today as
in the time of John and Jesus.

The land is stark and wild in the hills of Judea, and is
called a wilderness. Here John spent his youth in seclusion.

It is not known exactly how John was prepared for his
mission. He must have understood his destiny before the
world was. An angel ordained him when he was only eight
days old, and he was baptized while yet in his childhood.
What other heavenly messengers came to him can only be
guessed. The Bible says that as the child grew he became
strong in spirit. He must also have become strong in body to
survive the barren desert whose fearsome terrain was relieved

only by the soft green near the winding Jordan River.

As his sandals made little puffs of red dust crossing the rocky hills, John must have wondered sometimes if there would ever be anything for him but twisted olive trees stretching crooked arms to the blazing sky. And at night when the air chilled him until he shook with cold, did he dream of the ease of life in Jerusalem? Did he long for a simple meal prepared by Elisabeth as he searched the prickly brush for locusts? And when bees stung his hands and arms and face as he gathered honey to eat with the locusts that he roasted and ate, did he ever regret his call? John's only clothing was a rough coat of camel hair tied around the waist with a leather thong. Did he think sometimes of cool, smooth, silky robes to wear after a refreshing bath?

Whatever his thoughts might have been, his body became strong and his determination ever stronger as he grew in stature of mind and spirit and became worthy to prepare the way for the Messiah who was to come.

*John's
ministry
begins*

SOME PEOPLE HAVE WONDERED WHY THERE HAD TO BE A JOHN THE BAPTIST, AND ESPECIALLY WHY TWO OLD PEOPLE SHOULD BE CHOSEN TO BE HIS PARENTS. They have also wondered why a man of the desert who dressed in rough camelskin and leather should be the one to announce the birth of Jesus Christ. Why not angels sounding trumpets?

The answer to these questions lies in the name by which Gabriel said the son of Zacharias and Elisabeth should be called—John, John the Baptist—and that the prophets had foretold that he who prepared the people for the birth of Christ would be "the voice of one crying in the wilderness, Prepare ye the way of the Lord. . . ." (Mark 1:3.)

It was just as necessary for Jesus to be baptized, since he was born on earth, as for any other person who enters the kingdom of God, and to be baptized by immersion to represent the death of the old life and the beginning of a new. Jesus needed also to be baptized by one having authority from God, and John the Baptist held that authority.

We don't know how long John lived in the desert wilderness. He probably went there in his youth and dwelt there until he was about thirty years of age. This desert extended almost to Jerusalem, so it is possible that while he was in the wilds he knew something about the politics and other happenings in the nearby city. However, it is also possible that he lived like a hermit with heavenly messengers as his only teachers and companions.

The Jewish people had anxiously watched for a long time for a Messiah to come and free them from bondage and become their king. Prophets had foretold the birth of the King of the Jews for as long as anyone could remember. It was also said that the one who would be a witness of the Lamb of God, as John the Baptist was, should be of the proper lineage—of the house of Aaron.

Our Father in heaven knew that while the people had been warned many times of the birth of a Messiah, when the fulfillment of prophecy was close they would have to be warned again and taught to have some understanding of the meaning of the birth of Jesus Christ. And so John was born to Zacharias and Elisabeth, who were both descendants of Aaron.

When the Savior went to Bethlehem he was met by hostile people ready to attack and even to kill Him. He needed friends who would take His part and follow Him. These friends were gathered by John the Baptist. As the people listened to John's teachings, their hearts were prepared for the coming of Christ. And after they had repented of their sins their spirits were cleansed by baptism. John spoke of one greater than himself who would come after him, baptizing with fire and the Holy Ghost. He created an air of expectation. His followers watched and waited for the coming of the promised Messiah.

John teaches about baptism

A S JOHN NEARED HIS THIRTIETH BIRTHDAY, A HEAVENLY MESSENGER TOLD HIM THAT THE TIME HAD COME TO BEGIN HIS GREAT WORK. FOR ALMOST thirty years he had lived in the wilderness, waiting for the day when he could start his ministry. That day had at last arrived.

John's preparation had been thorough. He was prepared by our Heavenly Father while in the wilderness to be a champion of truth and right, and be a messenger for the coming of the Lord Jesus Christ.

When John reached the Jordan River and began to preach to the people, many wondered about him. "Could this

be the Messiah come at last?" some asked. "Did you see the length of his hair and the look in his eyes? He cannot be the Messiah," others declared.

Great crowds surrounded this handsome young man with his glowing countenance and stirring voice. Who among those who heard him could deny the excitement of his message? Who could forget his strong pleas to repent and do right? The Roman soldiers occupying the area became nervous over the influence John had on the people. The crowds seemed almost hypnotized by him and the words he spoke. They questioned his origin and wondered if he could be a spy sent by some powerful unknown king to overthrow the government. The Romans always suspected anyone with power of any kind, fearing he might try to take over their captured territory. John must be carefully watched, they decided.

"He that has two coats, let him give one to him that has none. And he that has extra meat—let him do likewise," John taught.

The Romans could not understand; they believed that no man in his right mind would give away a good coat or food to a stranger. *The man must be crazy,* they thought. *No wonder he dresses in those rough skins and forgets to cut his hair or trim his beard.*

But crazy or not, John attracted great crowds who were curious about his appearance, eager to hear his message. Why did listening to John make them feel so happy? As they tried to live his teachings by remembering the poor, turning from wickedness, and always trying to do right, they longed for the next step—baptism. Baptism by immersion for the remission of their sins! John's followers wanted to be washed clean.

WHEN JOHN APPEARED AS A PREACHER IN THE JUDEAN AREA, HE FEARED NO ONE. HE PROCLAIMED TO ALL the people, "Repent, for the kingdom of heaven is upon you." He was truly a voice crying in the wilderness as the prophet Isaiah had foretold.

With his rough camelskin clothing bound in leather, his long hair and wild beard, the light in his eyes and the fire in his voice, John attracted people from Jerusalem and all Judea. Hundreds came from across the entire Jordan valley to listen and learn and be baptized.

The Roman soldiers said, "We must stand in the crowds and guard against violence, for he looks to be a violent man."

John said to them, "Do violence to no man, neither accuse any falsely; and be content with your wages." The soldiers asked, "Who is this John who tries to teach Romans? Does he not know that the Roman legions are the finest in the world?" They watched and they listened.

When the tax collectors came to see what attracted the crowds, John told them never to collect more than was actually owed. "Why should this wild man tell us what to do?" they murmured. "We are entitled to all the money we can collect." But they, too, stayed to hear John.

Many people asked, "Is this the Christ?" They knew the Christ was soon to come, and there was a strange power in the message of John the Baptist.

John explained, "I indeed baptize you with water; but one mightier than I cometh, the latchet of whose shoes I am not worthy to unloose: he shall baptize you with the Holy Ghost and with fire." (Luke 3:16.)

Very few, if any, of John's listeners fully understood his message. As the Jordan River springs from the ground, seemingly coming from nowhere, so John seemed to have sprung from the wilderness.

Some thought he must be one of the Essenes who lived in settlements near the Dead Sea. Tales were told of these strange religious men who spent their time studying in their large library and copying sacred writings on scrolls that in our day would be known as the Dead Sea Scrolls. The Essenes cared little for the things of the world. They ate and dressed like John. Could he be one of these?

And if he were not the Messiah and not an Essene, who was he?

Isaiah's prophecy fulfilled

BAPTISM AS TAUGHT BY JOHN WAS NEW TO THE PEOPLE. THE JEWS BELIEVED THAT THEY WERE FORGIVEN OF THEIR SINS NOT BY BAPTISM BUT BY OFFERING SACRIFICES to God. So they brought bullocks, goats, oxen, lambs, doves—whatever they could afford—to be burned on the altars of the temple. They thought forgiveness came as the smoke rose into the air. Now John told them to repent and be baptized. Baptism had been reserved for the unclean

14

Gentiles who wished to become members of the tribe of
Israel. "The Jews be baptized? What could he mean?" they
questioned.

John baptized by immersion in the river Jordan. The
Jordan was an ideal place for a baptism, for its water was deep
enough to cover those to be baptized but it was not a swift
moving stream nor a dangerous one. On its shallow
banks tall trees provided shade from the blazing desert sun.
Crowds could sit in the cool shadows and listen to John's
ringing voice.

Every day John the Baptist preached repentance and
baptism to the people. Through his work the prophecy of
Isaiah was fulfilled. John performed baptisms with authority.
He was ordained by an angel when he was only eight days old
and given the power to overcome the kingdom of the Jews.

Jesus Himself would teach that unless a man be born of
the water and the Spirit he could not enter the kingdom of
God. As Christ was buried in the tomb following His
crucifixion, so those baptized must be buried under the water.
And as He came forth from the tomb in a newness of life, so
those who were baptized were brought forth from a symbolic
watery grave to their own new lives.

Many people who heard John were converted and
baptized. Others, such as the scribes and the elders, challenged
him. "Who are you? Are you the Messiah? Are you Elijah the
prophet? We must have an answer. Give an account of
yourself!"

And the humble preacher, John the Baptist, told them
that he had come to teach the gospel and to prepare the way
and bear witness of the Messiah.

The baptism of Jesus

WHEN JESUS "BEGAN TO BE ABOUT THIRTY YEARS OF AGE" AND WAS READY TO BEGIN HIS GREAT WORK, HE went first to John to be baptized. Jesus had been living in Galilee, a verdant and fertile cultivated land. Flowers carpeted the gently sloping hills. Wheat, barley, oranges, olives, and date palms flourished. The Sea of Galilee offered a rich crop to any fisherman willing to cast in his nets.

The time had come for the Son of God to leave familiar surroundings and journey along the shores of the Jordan. The river wound two hundred miles from the Sea of Galilee to empty into the Dead Sea, the lowest spot on earth. Somewhere on its banks He would find John the Baptist.

One sunny day at Bethany, John scanned the horizon and saw Jesus coming toward him. "Look," he cried, "there is the Lamb of God who taketh away the sins of the world. The reason that I came baptizing with water is so that He might be revealed to Israel."

For over thirty years John had been preparing for the time when he would baptize the Christ. All his life he had looked forward to this geat event. But when Jesus came to the Jordan to be baptized, John felt unworthy. He said humbly, "I have need to be baptized of Thee."

Jesus explained that everyone born on earth, even the Son of God, has need of baptism, which is a necessary ordinance as a symbol of conversion to the gospel. Then John

16

17

immersed Jesus in the Jordan River.

"And Jesus, when he was baptized, went up straightway out of the water: and, lo, the heavens were opened unto him, and he saw the Spirit of God descending like a dove, and lighting upon him: And lo a voice from heaven, saying, This is my beloved Son, in whom I am well pleased." (Matthew 3:16-17.)

John spoke and said, "I have seen the Spirit descend in the form of the dove and have heard a voice from heaven. I saw it myself and have borne witness. This is truly God's Chosen One."

The next day, while John was standing near the Jordan River with two of his disciples, Jesus walked by. John said, "Behold the Lamb of God." "And the two disciples heard him speak, and they followed Jesus." (John 1:36.)

One of the two was Andrew, brother of Simon Peter. Andrew was so sure that Jesus spoke the truth that he hurried to find his brother and tell him the good news. Soon many of John's followers turned to Jesus, the Messiah. John the Baptist had opened the Christian era for all time to come.

John in prison

JOHN THE BAPTIST CONTINUED HIS MINISTRY EVEN THOUGH JESUS HAD BEGUN TO TEACH AND GATHER DISCIPLES. JOHN WAS BAPTIZING NEAR SALIM BECAUSE THERE WAS MUCH water there. Puzzled people continued asking him about the man preaching on the other side of the Jordan.

18

"Who is He?" an old, bent, white-haired woman asked. "He is baptizing and crowds are flocking to Him."

John explained that Jesus was the Messiah. "I have been sent as His forerunner. You have heard me say that He is the Son of God. I am the Bridegroom's friend who is overjoyed at hearing the Bridegroom's voice. This joy, this perfect joy, is now mine. As He grows greater, I must grow less."

This was John's way of telling his followers that he had done his work to prepare the way for the Son of God; and as Jesus became more widely known and his influence more strongly felt, the need for John's testimony would decrease.

But John continued to be a strong prophet who did not hesitate to tell the truth. If he saw any person committing sin, even if the sinner was of royal blood, he quickly commanded that the person repent.

Herodias was a beautiful daughter of Aristobulus, son of Herod the Great. She had married her uncle Phillip, but left him and went to live with his half-brother Herod Antipas even though she had not been lawfully divorced from her husband.

John rebuked Herod, saying, "It is not lawful for thee to have thy brother's wife."

This made Herodias very angry. She hated John and "had a quarrel against him." She persuaded Herod to have John imprisoned for making such a statement about their so-called marriage.

Herodias would have been happy if Herod had immediately put John to death. But Herod was afraid that the people still thought of his prisoner as a prophet and would rebel and cause riots if an execution took place. Herod, too, almost believed that John was a holy man. Sometimes he had

20

his guards bring John to the throne room where he and the prisoner discussed affairs of the day and philosophy. Herod did not always understand John's teachings, but the Baptist fascinated the ruler. He recognized in John the mark of authority; like others, he seemed at times to be hypnotized by John's piercing eyes.

Herodias, however, hated John, and only his death could satisfy her. So she plotted with her daughter Salome to silence "the voice crying in the wilderness."

The wicked plan of Herodias

HERODIAS KNEW THAT HEROD WOULD INVITE HIS CHIEF OFFICIALS AND ARMY COMMANDERS AND MOST OF THE LEADING citizens of Galilee to celebrate his birthday by attending a big dinner. So she planned to have her daughter, Salome, dance before the guests.

The hall was prepared with lavish furnishings for the guests. The tables sagged with all the kinds of fruits to be found in the nearby country—oranges, bananas, apples, grapes, melons, dates, guavas, persimmons. There were meats, cheeses, breads, sweets, and every food imaginable. After the feast, Herodias arranged for her daughter's dance.

Salome was even more beautiful than her mother, and her dance entranced the guests. So pleased was Herod by it that he recklessly promised, and then swore an oath that he would keep this promise, to give her whatever she desired, even up to half his kingdom if she wished it.

Probably everyone at the feast tried to guess what Salome might request. They watched as she went to her mother for direction.

Herodias's only thought was revenge against John, who had shamed her and embarrassed her by telling the world about her sins and boldly declaring that her marriage to Herod was not moral or legal. So Herodias told Salome to demand that the head of John the Baptist be brought before her on a large silver platter!

Herod was "exceeding sorry." He knew that John was a just man and holy (Mark 6:20), and he did not want him killed. But he had promised before all the guests at the birthday feast that Salome could have anything she might ask. So he sent for an executioner and issued an order that John the Baptist should be killed and his head brought to the dining hall on a large silver tray.

And this was done!

When John's disciples heard of the tragedy, they hurried to the palace to claim his body. Herod Antipas, still regretting John's death, welcomed John's friends, who took away the body and quietly buried it. John had finished the work he had come to do. He had preached repentance and baptism to those who would listen. He was a valiant and great prophet whose whole life had been spent in the service of God.

From the time of the death of John the Baptist a shadow fell over the lives of Herod and his wife. He was later banished, and Herodias went with him to Gaul, where they both died.

John's mission continues

THE HISTORY OF JOHN THE BAPTIST DID NOT END ON THAT TRAGIC NIGHT WHEN HEROD ANTIPAS ORDERED HIS EXECUTION. NOR DID THE authority to baptize for the remission of sins—the Aaronic Priesthood—disappear forever with John's death.

While Joseph Smith and Oliver Cowdery were translating the Book of Mormon, they came upon references to baptism by immersion for the remission of sins. Because so many of the truths of the gospel had been lost to the world over the centuries, neither Joseph nor Oliver really knew what baptism by immersion for the remission of sins meant.

On May 15, 1829, as the two men knelt in the woods praying and inquiring for understanding of this baptism, "a messenger from heaven descended in a cloud of light, and having laid his hands upon us, he ordained us, saying: *Upon you my fellow servants, in the name of Messiah, I confer the Priesthood of Aaron, which holds the keys of the ministering of angels, and of the gospel of repentance, and of baptism by immersion for the remission of sins; and this shall never be taken again from the earth until the sons of Levi do offer again an offering unto the Lord in righteousness.*" (Joseph Smith—History 1:68-69.)

The messenger commanded Joseph to baptize Oliver, and Oliver to baptize Joseph. According to the angel's instruction, they baptized each other; then they ordained each other to the Aaronic Priesthood, also under his direction.

"The messenger who visited us on the occasion and

conferred this Priesthood upon us, said that his name was John, the same that is called John the Baptist in the New Testament. . . ." (Joseph Smith—History 1:72.)

After the two baptisms, Joseph and Oliver experienced the gift of prophecy and were filled with the Holy Ghost. Through this new priesthood, they were able to understand more clearly the true meaning of certain difficult passages of scripture.

John the Baptist prepared the way for the first coming of Christ. As a heavenly messenger, he was instrumental in the opening of a new dispensation for the second coming of the Savior. Both advents had been foretold by the prophets from the beginning. And John's priesthood, the Priesthood of Aaron, is again on earth and will be until Christ Himself shall come as King of kings and Lord of lords to reign for a thousand years.